First Facts

Water in Our World

Saving Water

by Rebecca Olien

CAPSTONE PRESS
a capstone imprint

First Facts are published by Capstone Press,
1710 Roe Crest Drive, North Mankato, Minnesota 56003
www.capstonepub.com

Library of Congress Cataloging-in-Publication Data
Olien, Rebecca, author.
  Saving water / by Rebecca Olien. — [New edition]
     pages cm. — (First facts. Water in our world)
  Summary: "Describes the sources of freshwater on Earth and ways people can conserve water"—Provided by
publisher.
  Audience: Ages 7-9
  Audience: K to grade 3
  Includes bibliographical references and index.
  ISBN 978-1-4914-8279-7 (library binding)
  ISBN 978-1-4914-8283-4 (paperback)
  ISBN 978-1-4914-8287-2 (eBook PDF)
  1. Water conservation—Juvenile literature. I. Title.
  TD495.O45 2016
  333.91′16—dc2
                    2015026112

Editorial Credits
Abby Colich, editor; Kyle Grenz, designer; Wanda Winch, media researcher; Laura Manthe,
production specialist

Photo Credits
Capstone Studio: Karon Dubke, 13; Getty Images, Inc: Justin Sullivan, 9; The Pajaro Valley Water Management
Agency: Shinehah Bigham, 14; Shutterstock: Baloncici, 10, Chaoss, 18-19, Cylonphoto, 17, Ecelop, waves design,
Migel, 7, Riccardo Mayer, 5, shao weiwei, 20, SKY2015, 1, tachyglossus, splash design, YuryZap, cover

Printed in China.
007480RRDS16

Table of Contents

Sharing Water 4

Freshwater 6

Laws Protect Water 8

Businesses Save Water 11

Saving Water at Home 12

Saving Water Outdoors 15

Reusing Water 16

Saving Water 19

Amazing But True! 20
Hands On: Removing Salt 21

Glossary 22
Read More 23
Internet Sites 23
Critical Thinking Using the Common Core . . . 24
Index 24

Sharing Water

All living things must share Earth's water. People, plants, and animals need water to live. Only a small amount of Earth's water is safe for people to use. People need to save water by using less.

Fact!

About 783 million people around the world cannot easily get clean water.

Freshwater

Many people think there is enough water on Earth. *Salt water* in oceans makes up 97 percent of Earth's water. But people can't drink salt water.

Only 3 percent of Earth's water is *freshwater*. Most freshwater is frozen in *glaciers*. People can use only the freshwater from lakes, rivers, and *aquifers*.

salt water—water that is salty; salt water is found in oceans
freshwater—water that has little or no salt; most ponds, rivers, lakes, and streams have freshwater
glacier—a large sheet of frozen freshwater; glaciers are found in mountains and polar areas
aquifer—an underground lake

Laws Protect Water

Many laws help protect water. Some laws protect freshwater sources. Other laws help keep water clean. Some places have laws to *limit* when people can water lawns and gardens.

limit—to keep within a certain amount; laws help save water by limiting how much people can use

BROWN
is the new GREEN
We´re doing our part to conserve
water during this drought.

f ♥ #DroughtSF   Request a sign: sfwater.org/conservation

Businesses Save Water

Businesses use millions of gallons of water. Factories use water to make items such as paper, cars, and other goods. Power plants use water to make electricity.

Many businesses save water by reusing it. Some car washes save soapy water in underground tanks. The water is cleaned and reused to wash other cars.

Saving Water at Home

People can save water at home. To save water, turn off the faucet when brushing your teeth. Take shorter showers.

People can save water at home in other ways. Fixing leaky toilets and faucets saves water. Using more *efficient* dishwashers and washing machines also saves water.

efficient—not wasteful of time or energy

Irrigated with recycled water

🚱 Not for drinking

Pajaro Valley Water
Management Agency

14

Saving Water Outdoors

Farmers use water to grow crops. To save water, some farmers grow crops that need less water. Other farmers use water that cities *recycle* on their crops.

At home people use the most water outdoors. To save water, people should only water lawns when needed. Using sprinklers in the evening instead of during the daytime also saves water.

recycle—to use something again

Reusing Water

People can reuse water in many ways. Rainwater and waste from sinks and toilets collect in *sewers*. *Water treatment plants* clean the water from the sewers. People can then drink the new clean water and use it in their homes.

sewer—an underground pipe that carries away waste water

water treatment plant—a place where water is cleaned for people to use at home

water treatment plant

Saving Water

Saving water helps make sure all living things have the freshwater they need. People, plants, and animals share the same freshwater. Everyone must work together to save water and keep it clean.

Fact!

A dripping faucet can waste 20 gallons (76 liters) of water a day.

Amazing But True!

How would you like a cold glass of ocean water? Scientists can remove the salt from ocean water. Ocean water is heated or pushed through a filter to remove the salt. People can drink the water once the salt is removed.

Hands On: Removing Salt

Scientists heat ocean water to remove the salt. Try this experiment to see how hot salt water can become freshwater.

What You Need

- 2 teaspoons (10 grams) salt
- clean jar with lid
- hot water

What You Do

1. Place the salt in the jar.
2. Fill the jar half full with hot water from the faucet.
3. Cover the jar with the lid.
4. Wait 10 minutes.
5. Notice the drops of water forming on the sides and lid of the jar. Carefully remove the lid. Taste the drops on the inside of the lid. Do they taste salty? The water on the lid is evaporated fresh water. The salt stays behind in the jar.

Glossary

aquifer (AK-wuh-fuhr)—an underground lake

efficient (uh-FI-shuhnt)—not wasteful of time or energy

freshwater (FRESH-WAH-tur)—water that has little or no salt; most ponds, rivers, lakes, and streams have freshwater

glacier (GLAY-shur)—a large sheet of frozen freshwater; glaciers are found in mountains and polar areas

limit (LIM-it)—to keep within a certain amount; laws help save water by limiting how much people can use

recycle (ree-SYE-kuhl)—to use something again

salt water (SAWLT WAH-tur)—water that is salty; salt water is found in oceans

sewer (SOO-ur)—an underground pipe that carries away waste water

water treatment plant (WAH-tur TREET-muhnt PLANT)—a place where water is cleaned for people to use at home

Read More

Ditchfield, Christin. *The Story Behind Water*. True Stories. Chicago: Heinemann Library, 2012.

Green, Jen. *Saving Water*. Environment Detective Investigates. New York: Windmill Books, 2012.

Mulder, Michelle. *Every Last Drop: Bringing Clean Water Home*. Victoria, Canada: Orca Book Publishers, 2014.

Internet Sites

FactHound offers a safe, fun way to find Internet sites related to this book. All of the sites on FactHound have been researched by our staff.

Here's all you do:

Visit *www.facthound.com*

Type in this code: 9781491482797

Check out projects, games and lots more at
www.capstonekids.com

Critical Thinking Using the Common Core

1. Why should people try to not waste water? (Key Idea and Details)
2. Using online or print resources, list three ways to save water that are not mentioned in the book. (Integration of Knowledge and Ideas)
3. Reread page 16 and look at the photo on page 17. Which side is the untreated water from sewers? Which side is the treated water that people can drink? (Craft and Structure)

Index

animals, 4, 19
aquifers, 6

businesses, 10–11

crops, 14–15

Earth, 4, 6,

factories, 11, 15
farmers, 15
freshwater, 6, 8, 19

glaciers, 6
homes, 12–13, 16–17

lakes, 6
laws, 8

oceans, 6, 20

people, 6, 8, 12, 15, 16, 19, 20
plants, 4, 15, 19
power plants, 11

reusing water, 11, 15, 16–17
rivers, 6

salt water, 6, 20
sewers, 16

watering lawns, 8, 15